FROGS and TOADS
AS A NEW PET

W9-BLR-445

JOHN COBORN

CONTENTS

Photography: William B. Allen, Jr.: 15, 25; G. Baumgart: 47, 58; John Coborn: 44; M.J. Cox: 59; George Dibley: 4, 5, 11, 60, 62; Dr. Guido Dingerkus: 8, 21, 29, 63; F.J. Dodd, Jr.: 49; Jeff Gee: 24; Michael Gilroy: 18, 19, 23, 27, 32, 40, 56; Burkhard Kahl: 41, 61; J.K. Langhammer: 31, 43; Ken Lucas, Steinhart Aquarium: 3, 30, 34, 35, 37, 39, 45, 50, 51, 57; Elaine Radford: 9; Ivan Sazima: 36; Harald Schultz: 7; Lothar Wischnath: 17, 20, 33, 46, 48 bottom; Robert T. Zappalorti: 2, 13, 53, 54, 55; Ruda Zukal: 6.

Inside front cover: *Pelobates fuscus*; photo by Karl H. Switak.
Inside back cover: *Boophis difficilis*; photo by Paul Freed.

987654321   **1996 Edition**   95 789

Distributed in the UNITED STATES to the Pet Trade by T.F.H. Publications, Inc., One T.F.H. Plaza, Neptune City, NJ 07753; distributed in the UNITED STATES to the Bookstore and Library Trade by National Book Network, Inc. 4720 Boston Way, Lanham MD 20706; in CANADA to the Pet Trade by H & L Pet Supplies Inc.; 27 Kingston Crescent, Kitchener, Ontario N2B 2T6; Rolf C. Hagen Ltd., 3225 Sartelon Street, Montreal 382 Quebec; in CANADA to the Book Trade by Vanwell Publishing Ltd., 1 Northrup Crescent, St. Catharines, Ontario L2M 6P5 ; in ENGLAND by T.F.H. Publications, PO Box 15, Waterlooville PO7 6BQ; in AUSTRALIA AND THE SOUTH PACIFIC by T.F.H. (Australia), Pty. Ltd., Box 149, Brookvale 2100 N.S.W., Australia; in NEW ZEALAND by Brooklands Aquarium Ltd. 5 McGiven Drive, New Plymouth, RD1 New Zealand; in Japan by T.F.H. Publications, Japan—Jiro Tsuda, 10-12-3 Ohjidai, Sakura, Chiba 285 Japan in SOUTH AFRICA by Lopis (Pty) Ltd., P.O. Box 39127, Booysens, 2016 Johannesburg, South Africa. Published by T.F.H. Publica-

Facts about Frogs and Toads

Pine Barrens tree frog, *Hyla andersoni*, posing with a suitable prop.

Frogs and toads (order Anura, which literally means "no tail") are members of the zoological class Amphibia, which they share with the salamanders and newts (order Caudata) and the little known, limbless caecilians (order Gymnophiona). In recent years, zoologists have given increased attention to amphibian species which, compared with the birds and mammals for example, have been somewhat neglected in the past.

Being mainly nocturnal, secretive and often confined to remote areas, many species of frogs and toads are difficult to find. However, recent dedicated research by a number of herpetologists specializing in amphibians has led to the discovery of many new species; these, no doubt, will be joined by many more in the next few years. The most complete, up-to-date catalogue of living amphibian species is *Amphibian Species of the World*, published in 1985, compiled by a number of eminent experts and coordinated and edited by Darrel R. Frost. Published jointly by Allen Press and the Association of Systematics Collections (Lawrence, Kansas, USA), this mammoth work lists 4014 nominal species of amphibians, of which 3507 are frogs and toads, making the anurans by far the largest group. It is a conservative estimate to say that at least 200 new species of amphibian have been described or proposed since the publication of this important work—and it will be some considerable time before our knowledge of the class will be complete.

On cursory inspection, all species of frogs and toads are similar in shape. Squat in form, with long powerful hindlegs used for jumping and swimming; usually (but not always) webbed toes and sometimes webbed fingers; all species completely lack a tail (with the exception of the "tailed frog," *Ascaphus truei*, but this is not really a tail at all, but an extension of the vent, which is used as a copulatory organ).

The life history of the average frog is known by every school child. For a long time, frogs or toads have been standard material used in the teaching of biology for both behavioral and anatomical studies. In this little book, we are more concerned about keeping frogs alive and well and breeding them than in studying their insides, so it is important that we know what "makes them tick" and what influences their breeding cycles.

Let us first try to explain what the difference is between a frog and a toad. In fact, there is no real hard and fast distinction. The two

Albino bullfrog, *Rana catesbeiana*. Members of this species have been known to establish territories that they will defend by engaging in vicious brawls.

words originated in England (which does not have many species of frogs and toads), where "frog" was used for those with a smooth, wet skin and "toad" was used for the dry, warty ones. Thus members of the genus *Rana* were frogs, and members of the genus *Bufo* were toads. However, large numbers of species have since been discovered which fit into neither category. To get around this, experts use the word anuran (from Anura) to generalize frog or toad, or sometimes they just use the word frog for both types.

Being amphibians, anurans typically (but not always) require bodies of fresh water in which to reproduce. No frog is capable of surviving in sea water, though a few species can tolerate a mild, brackish water. A typical life history is that of the North American northern leopard frog, *Rana pipiens*. Favorable changes in climatic conditions in early spring, when temperatures begin to rise and the days begin to lengthen, will bring the frogs out of hibernation. Although not one of the more vocal anurans, male leopard frogs will congregate at suitable bodies of water and emit their comical song, consisting of a low gutteral snort followed by a number of clucking notes. The song is designed to attract female frogs and to repel males. There is often considerable jostling among males (which may outnumber the females by as many as three to one) to gain the attention of a female. Eventually, every female will be grasped by a male, his arms around the body just below her forelimbs, in a characteristic embrace technically known as amplexus. The grip is very strong and aided by dark roughened areas on the males' thumbs, known as nuptial pads. These pads are most evident during the breeding season and are barely discernible at other times.

The pairing stimulates the female to lay her eggs. As many as six.thousand may be laid in clumps, which are attached to submerged plants or simply placed on the substrate. Each tiny, spherical, velvety-black egg is less than .5 mm in diameter, and as the eggs are being laid the male fertilizes them with a stream of spermal fluid. Each egg is surrounded by a substance which rapidly absorbs water and forms a thick jelly-like, protective capsule. After pairing and laying, the parents show no further interest in the eggs and eventually leave the water to hunt for insects and other vertebrates in the surrounding vegetation.

Within hours of being laid, development of the eggs begins. Each original egg is a single cell, but this soon divides to form two cells; these divide to form four and so on. Within three days the shape of the developing tadpole can be

One of the red-eyed tree frogs, *Agalychnis annae*. Some experts believe that members of this genus are too delicate to make good pets; others believe that these frogs are quite hardy if given adequate temperature, humidity, and ventilation.

seen. As it grows, the tadpole is nourished by the yolk part of the egg. On the eighth or ninth day, the tadpole "hatches" from the jelly-like capsule and clings to the jelly mass or to waterplants by a pair of sticky, sucker-like appendages just below the mouth. The tail is well-developed and tiny, external gills are discernible on either side of the head. By the

some tadpoles become carnivorous, feeding on carrion or small aquatic organisms.

For the next four weeks or so, the tadpoles feed almost constantly and grow rapidly from about 8 to 26 mm (.3 to 1 in). During this time, each tadpole lives a life of extreme danger and many fall prey to carnivorous water creatures, from fish to garter snakes and

Amplexus in African clawed frogs, *Xenopus laevis*. Albinism occasionally occurs in this species.

sixteenth day, a cover has grown over the gills, which are now internal, almost like those of a fish. The yolk sac, on which the tadpole has been nourished for the first few days of its life, is absorbed, and the little creature must now actively seek out a food supply. The tadpoles of most frog species feed initially on humus and vegetable matter such as algae, which they can scrape from surfaces of rocks, plants, etc., with their horny and rasping lips. Later,

from dragonfly larvae to giant water beetles. The hindlimbs begin to develop first, then the forelimbs. The appetite diminishes temporarily as the tail begins to be absorbed and the body of a froglet begins to form. For another few weeks, the little frogs stay in the water, migrating to the pond's edge in July or August, where they live among the vegetation, feeding on tiny insects and other invertebrates. As they may still fall prey to birds, snakes, turtles and other carnivores, they are extremely wary and dive for cover at the slightest disturbance, their cryptic coloration affording them excellent camouflage under the floating vegetation.

As it grows, the leopard frog will venture onto land away from the water's edge but will always favor damp spots and places where it can quickly make for the safety of water should it be threatened. The frogs eat as much as they can in order to get them through the lean times of winter.

Thus we have a brief summary of the life history of a "typical" species. However, of the 3500 or more known species there are many that have lifecycles and habits which are far from typical. Although most frogs and toads, with their moist skin, are prone to desiccation and are therefore confined to moist habitats, many species have radiated into the most surprisingly diverse habitats, ranging from the peaks of the mountains to arid deserts and from the edge of the arctic circle to the tops of trees at the equator. Frequently, the mode of reproduction reflects the habitat. Some desert species lay buried in a capsule for months at a time, only being released by sudden downpours of a desert storm. Then in a frenzy of activity the frogs have to mate and lay eggs as fast as they can—the full cycle has to

take place in a short time before the temporary water pools all dry up again. Some tropical tree-dwelling species lay a small number of eggs in a water-filled hollow in a tree branch or in the water store of a pitcher plant or bromeliad. In some species parental care is highly developed, to the extent that adults carry the eggs or tadpoles around on their backs until they find a suitable "nursery pond." Other species build foam nests on the end of branches overhanging a body of water, into which the tadpoles drop when they hatch. There are frogs which carry tadpoles around in little chambers on their backs, from which miniature replicas of the adults eventually "hatch." There is even a gastric brooding frog, which is unique in the animal kingdom in that it swallows its fertilized eggs, converts its stomach to a "uterus" and eventually gives birth to fully formed young through its mouth!

Brazilian orange tree frog, *Hyla punctata*. Members of the genus *Hyla* are well-known for their loud and prolonged mating calls.

Housing

If you intend to keep frogs or toads, the accommodations required must be planned well in advance; it is bad policy to acquire the animals first and then start worrying about housing them. In most cases it is best to keep each species in separate accomodation, not only so that differences in habitat or habits can be catered to, but because some species are unable to withstand the temperament and/or the body secretions of others! In addition, some species will not only eat other species almost as large as themselves, they may even eat their own brothers and sisters!

TYPES OF ACCOMMODATIONS

A container in which living animals are kept is called an aquarium, a terrarium or an aqua-terrarium. The first is used for keeping totally aquatic species, the second for terrestrial (land-dwelling) species and the third for partly terrestrial (amphibious) species. By far the greatest number of amphibians fall into the last category, as most require water in which to breed. In addition to knowing whether your chosen species is aquatic, terrestrial or partly terrestrial, you should know something about its habits and native habitat so that you can provide as near natural conditions as possible.

The Aquarium: An aquarium tank can be used as an aquarium, a terrarium or an aqua-terrarium, but in this section we are dealing with an aquarium for totally aquatic species (*Xenopus* or *Pipa* for example) where no land area is required. There are many kinds of aquarium tanks available on the market, from the somewhat old-fashioned steel-framed glass tanks, to clear plastic and all-glass. The latter are by far the most satisfactory and decorative, at least for display tanks; other kinds can be used for breeding, rearing, quarantine, etc. The all-glass tank consists of glass panels cemented together along the edges with a remarkably versatile substance known as silicone-rubber sealing compound. Such aquaria can be purchased ready-made, you can have one built to your specifications, or you can quite easily make one yourself.

The dimensions of the tank will depend on the number and size of the frogs you wish to keep, but it is wise to keep a minimum size of 60 cm long by 30 cm wide by 30 cm deep (2 x 1 x 1 ft). Such a size would be suitable for a pair of Surinam toads (*Pipa pipa*) or similar species. Remember that a tank full of water is very weighty; in the size mentioned above the water alone will weigh 54 kg (approximately 120 lbs or over 1 cwt), and to this we have to add the weight of the tank itself plus substrate and decoration materials (gravel and rocks are even heavier than water). Thus we have to ensure that the base on which the tank is kept is very sturdily constructed and preferably reinforced with steel.

For display purposes, it is good to create an environment in the tank which is as natural looking as possible. Try to picture the sort of environment in which your chosen species lives in the wild. However, it is necessary to use compromises

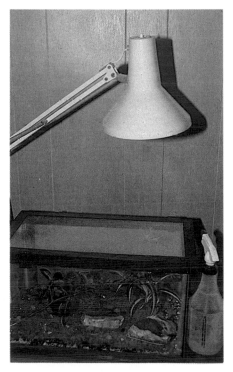

Example of a simple terrarium used to house very hardy amphibians. Housing for pet frogs must take into account the specific needs of the animals in question.

9

in many cases—river mud, for example, should be substituted with gravel—for obvious reasons. For setting up an aquascape for frogs, you will obtain many interesting tips from books about tropical or coldwater fishkeeping. Here it will suffice to say that a layer of washed aquarium gravel about 5 cm (2 in) deep at the front, sloping up to 7.5 cm (3 in) at the rear (deeper for larger tanks) should be placed on the floor of the tank.

For decorative purposes, you can use a few non-toxic rocks or river pebbles (granite, slate, etc., but limestone should be avoided) placed to form caves, valleys and terraces. Pieces of treated bogwood can also be used to good effect. For small aquatic frogs and tadpoles, you can cultivate waterplants in the substrate, but the continual grubbing actions of some of the larger species may make this a waste of time. The best method is to use only robust plants which are allowed to develop a stable root system before the animals are introduced.

The Aqua-terrarium: Most amphibian species require an aqua-terrarium with a varying ratio of land to water depending on the species being kept, although in most cases roughly half land and half water will be adequate. An aqua-terrarium is also ideal for breeding many species and is especially useful for rearing tadpoles to their terrestrial stage. An all-glass aquarium tank can be used, with the addition of a glass partition, about 15 cm (6 in) high, cemented (with the aforesaid sealer) across the bottom of the tank to make a waterproof barrier between the land and the water. The water area can be given a 2.5 cm (1 in) thick layer of fine grade aquarium gravel, thus giving a water depth of 12.5 cm (5 in). To provide easy exit from the water, a gradient of rocks and pebbles can be placed up the side of the glass partition.

The land area is half-filled with stones and coarse gravel to provide drainage (ideally a drainage hole should be incorporated into the floor of this area), then a mixture of sterilized garden loam, peat and coarse sand (commercial potting mix is ideal) is placed on top to fill in the area and to slope up and away from the water. A slab of turf or pieces of moss may be placed over this, coupled with mossy bark or stones to form hiding places. Plants are preferably left in their pots so that they can be changed easily (it is often difficult to get plants to fare well in a terrarium, so keep two sets so that they can be given regular periods of "rest and recreation"). The pots can be sunk into the substrate or concealed behind rocks, bark, etc. If possible, use plants which are compatible with the conditions in the tank and, for authenticity, try and get plant species which come from the same part of the world as your frogs.

If you are ambitious (and can afford it), it is possible to construct a built-in aqua-terrarium in an alcove of your house or conservatory. Such a display can have a concrete, fiberglass or plastic pond, waterfalls, built-in humidity sprinklers, etc. The back wall of the display can be built up with mossy rocks, and cavities between them can be filled with potting compost to take lush tropical plants. The whole unit is enclosed behind framed glass doors, with fine mesh (insect screening) panels above for ventilation. With careful and artistic planning, you can create an attractive, natural-looking indoor section of tropical rainforest in which your frogs will really feel at home and will be likely to breed without any problems.

The Terrarium: The terrarium is a container constructed for species which are totally or almost totally terrestrial and is usually taller than it is long. It is ideal for frogs which spend much of their time in the tree canopy and which do not require large volumes of water in which to breed (*Dendrobates* species, for example). A glass-fronted, timber construction may be used, but as you are likely to require a high humidity it is usually best to have a specially constructed all-glass tank or a mixture of glass and acrylic sheeting (plexiglass). The advantages of the latter are that they can be easily drilled and shaped and are ideal as sliding

Aquariums and terrariums housing frogs and toads can be made more decorative through the use of decorative scenes, available at pet shops, that attach to the housing unit; the scenes also can help to cut down on the amount of light (and visual distraction) coming from outside the unit.

ventilation panels to be affixed in one or more sides. The main panels should be of high-quality glass so that crystal clear viewing is possible.

A suitable size for a group of dendrobatids (approximately six) would be 50 x 50 x 75 cm tall (20 x 20 x 30 in). A layer of clean gravel is placed in the base, and this can be covered with slabs of living moss (which may have to be changed regularly). A dead tree branch is placed in the center of the substrate, and this can be decorated with living epiphytic plants. In addition, or alternatively, a potted climbing plant can be used to provide extra interest and cover for the frogs.

Greenhouses: Many tropical and subtropical species can be kept in greenhouses, providing you are able to maintain adequate temperatures throughout the year and remembering that during a power failure for a few hours in the winter, all your efforts may be lost (it is well worth investing in an emergency heating system if you ever intend to go into frog-keeping in a big way). However, there are some great advantages in keeping frogs in a greenhouse. If you provide them with the correct facilities, they will breed in almost natural conditions. This applies especially to some of the larger species which require deep waters with relatively large surface areas.

Deep water tanks or artificial ponds can be let into the floor of the greenhouse. Beware of overheating in the summer—you must have adequate ventilation facilities. Any windows which open should of course be covered with insect screening to prevent the inmates from escaping.

The Outdoor Enclosure: Native species and those from a similar climate can be kept in outdoor ponds or enclosures. Once you have built a pond, put a wall around it (preferably with an overhang at the top to prevent escapes) and landscaped the land area, you have little else to do, as the frogs will virtually look after themselves. They will find most of their own food, though it will do no harm to feed them individually with a few mealworms at regular intervals. Providing the conditions are to their liking, your frogs will breed readily in such an outdoor enclosure.

LIFE SUPPORT SYSTEMS

In addition to the terrarium and its decorations, there are a number of life support items to be taken into consideration. These include temperature, lighting, ventilation and humidity. Let us examine each of these items individually.

Heating: Temperature requirements of frogs and toads will vary, depending on where a particular species originates. If you live in a cold climate and you wish to keep tropical frogs, then it is obvious that your terrarium will require some form of supplementary heating to provide optimum temperatures for the species in question. Conversely, some of the temperate and cold weather species may require some form of cooling if kept in warmer climates. Of course, if you keep species native to the area in which you live, then you will get by without warming or cooling.

One of the most satisfactory means of heating a terrarium is to use the aquarium heaters which are normally supplied for tropical fish tanks. There are many makes, sizes and strengths available from pet shops and aquarist suppliers, but most consist of a heating element and a thermostat housed in a toughened glass tube with a waterproof stopper through which the power cable passes. The thermostat can be set so that a constant temperature is achieved. To heat the water in an aquarium, the heater is simply placed in the water. In an aqua-terrarium, the heater will also increase the temperature of the airspace as well as improve humidity; while in the dry terrarium, the heater can be simply placed in a concealed container of water where it will act as a heater and humidifier.

At one time an ordinary domestic lightbulb was the standard form of heating for a small terrarium. Indeed there is certainly nothing wrong with using these lamps; they are cheap and come in various sizes. By experimenting with the wattages, you will come up with the optimum temperature. One disadvantage is that tropical species requiring constant day and night temperatures will be inflicted with "continuous daylight" unless you use a blue or red bulb. If you require the bulb to light the terrarium during the day, the answer is to have two bulbs, a clear one for daytime and a colored one for night-time.

Heat lamps should be used with caution, as the amount of radiant heat they emit can be dangerous to both plants and animals. If used, the lamp should be preferably placed outside the tank and directed through the gauze or mesh

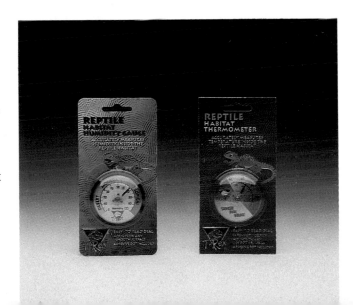

in the lid. The correct temperature can be achieved by experimentally moving the lamp up or down. Other forms of heating which may be considered include heating cables and heating pads. They are used by horticulturists to provide "bottom heat" for the plants. The former can be passed through the substrate; the latter are placed under the terrarium.

As frogs and toads are ectothermic, they adjust their body temperatures by moving among a range of external temperatures (this applies mainly to terrestrial species or species during their terrestrial stage and not so much to aquatic species where constant temperatures are more the norm). Each species has its own preferred optimum temperature. To allow captive amphibians to select their own preferred temperatures in the confines of the terrarium, it is advisable to have a range of temperatures. This is easily achieved by having the heating apparatus at one end of the terrarium only; the warmest area will then be near the heater, and the temperature will reduce gradually with the distance away from it. The frogs will then be able to select a spot to sit where they feel most comfortable.

In most climatic areas there is a temperature drop at night; this may be as little as 3°C (5°F) in low level equatorial areas, but can be as much as 20°C (36°F) or more in montane, continental or temperate climates. Most species will benefit from a compromise reduction in temperature of 5–10°C (9–18°F) at night. This can be achieved by simply switching off the heater each evening and switching it on again each morning. The prevailing room temperature in the average house will be okay for most frogs and toads at night. Seasonal variations in temperature must also be taken into consideration. Most species' breeding cycles are affected one way or another by seasonal climatic changes, so reduced winter temperatures are important for many species.

Lighting: Most species of frog and toad are nocturnal and/or crepuscular, and even those that are active during the day tend to move about in areas of heavy shade. This, however, does not mean that lighting is unimportant to our amphibians. As with most animals, the biorhythms of frogs and toads are affected by photoperiod (daily duration of light). Many species rest during the day and know that it is time to become active as the sun goes down. Seasonal changes of photoperiod outside the tropics are also important to many species, and most temperate species come into breeding condition when influenced by increasing lengths of

daylight as well as by a gradual rise in temperature.

Successful breeding of your amphibians will only occur when you try to reproduce the dark/light cycle of its native habitat. If more than one species is kept in the terrarium (which often is not a good idea), try to choose species that come from similar habitats and climatic areas. It is best to use artificial lighting in indoor terraria, as natural sunlight entering through glass will soon produce lethal temperatures unless the greatest of care is taken.

If your terrarium plants are to flourish, it is essential that the artificial light source you use is of the highest quality. Ongoing experiments with broad spectrum (artificial daylight) type light sources have produced some excellent systems. Horticultural lamps and fluorescent tubes which emit a quality of light ideal for plant growth are now available. The lamps come in all sorts of sizes, shapes and wattages, and you will be able to find something suitable for every type of terrarium. Fluorescent tubes can be mounted on brackets, behind gauze (to protect the inmates) in the aquarium lid; lamps which tend to emit a great deal of heat should be placed outside the terrarium and directed through a gauze or mesh screen.

Ventilation and Humidity: These are closely tied in with each other. If you have high humidity without ventilation, then the air in the terrarium will soon become foul and mold will develop on the substrate, bacteria will flourish,

15

and there is a good chance that your animals will get sick. Conversely, if you have too much ventilation and not enough humidity, the air will dry out very quickly, posing another danger to your moist-skinned charges.

Good ventilation will prevent a build-up of foul, organism-laden air and remove excess carbon dioxide, while adequate humidity will ensure that your frogs flourish. The terrarium should have ventilation grilles in the sides, as low down as possible, and in the lid. This will allow all of the air in the container to be exchanged constantly. If you have a heater, the convection currents created will speed up ventilation. An aerator in the water part of the terrarium will not only provide additional ventilation but will also help maintain a high humidity in the air. Humidity can also be increased by regular (at least twice a day) mist spraying. Living plants will themselves help to keep the humidity high, as well as contribute to keeping the air fresh.

Filtration: The very habits of aquatic and semi-aquatic frogs mean that they are rather messy and will soon pollute the water in an aquarium or aqua-terrarium. This means that the water will have to be changed rather frequently or you will have to install a filter. As it is not advisable to disturb your animals too frequently, it is better to take the latter course. The simplest type of filter is known as a box filter and is operated by an air pump. It consists (usually) of a plastic box filled loosely with a filter medium such as nylon wool. It works on the principle that rising air bubbles create a current in the water. The airline (usually with a small airstone attached) is placed at the bottom of the tube in the center of the filter. The rising air bubbles will create a current up the tube, and replacement water will have to flow through the filter medium where suspended materials are removed. The filter medium is quite easy to change at regular intervals, and such a filter is quite adequate for small volumes of water, especially if, say, at weekly intervals part of the water is changed (for example, remove ten cupfuls and replace with a similar amount; this provides much less disturbance than completely replacing all of the water every few days).

For larger volumes of water it is best to use a power filter. There are many commercial types manufactured primarily for fish-keepers. They consist of a relatively large pump which removes water from the tank, forces it through a filter chamber, and then returns it to the tank. For more details on such filters you are advised to consult your suppliers.

"Good ventilation will prevent a build-up of foul, organism-laden air and remove excess carbon dioxide, while adequate humidity will ensure that your frogs flourish."

Foods and Feeding

All animals, no matter what kind, require a balanced diet in order to stay in prime condition. A balanced diet is one that contains proteins, carbohydrates, fats, vitamins and minerals in a ratio suitable for the animal in question. Different animals acquire their balanced diet in different ways, but frogs and toads are totally carnivorous (with the exception of the tadpoles of many species which may be wholly or partly vegetarian), feeding on a variety of invertebrates or, in the case of some of the larger species, small vertebrates. It is the variety which ensures that the animal gets all of its requirements and, of course, if herbivorous creatures are consumed by frogs, the latter will receive a possibly beneficial proportion of vegetable material in the diet in a roundabout way.

To the keeper of frogs and toads, which seem to have an almost unlimited appetite, one of the biggest headaches can be the provision of an adequate supply and variety of food items in the correct sizes. Most frogs will take only livefood, and it is the movement of the creatures which actually provokes a feeding response (though aquatic species may also rely on the senses of touch and smell, which explains why they will take carrion in the wild or strips of meat in captivity). There are a number of commercially raised invertebrates which can be purchased. You can also start your own cultures of various food items, which will save you money as well as provide you with a ready supply of food at all times.

COLLECTING LIVEFOODS

One of the most satisfactory ways of providing a variety of invertebrates for your amphibians is to collect items from the wild. Not only will this relieve the "boredom" which can arise from a monotonous supply of cultured foodstuffs, but it will also most certainly introduce additional beneficial nutrients to your frogs' diet.

Perhaps the most productive method of collecting a variety of terrestrial insects and spiders is by "sweeping" herbage with a canvas-reinforced sweepnet. The mouth of the net is simply swept through the foliage of trees, shrubs and tall grass, and the resulting catch is placed in plastic containers for transport home. During the summer months, such sweepings will provide you with a great variety of caterpillars, grasshoppers, beetles, bugs, spiders, etc. After grading into suitable sizes, these various invertebrates will be eagerly taken by your frogs. Do not introduce too many insects at a time into the terrarium; allow one lot to be devoured before adding the next or you will get escapees into the house or the insects will drown in the water and spoil.

Giant mealworm beetle. Mealworms, a popular terrarium food item, are the larvae of these beetles.

You may want to invest in a flytrap; several designs are available commercially or you may try making your own. You can also find a variety of invertebrates by turning over logs and rocks, etc., where you will be sure to capture pillbugs, beetles, earthworms, slugs and snails. Many small flies and beetles congregate in flowerheads; these are very suitable for small frog species and newly metamorphosed youngsters. They can be collected with a glass bottle topped with a cork through which two glass tubes are passed. In one tube, the mouthpiece is bent over at right angles and passes just through the cork; the other tube is straight but passes near the bottom of the bottle. On its outer end, a piece of flexible rubber tubing is attached. The end of this tubing is placed near the insects to be collected and they are captured by sucking sharply on the mouthpiece. They

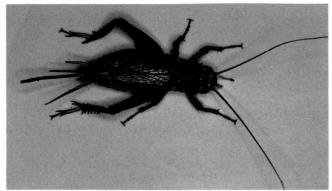

will be drawn through the glass tube into the bottle. A piece of wadding placed in the mouthpiece will prevent you from accidentally inhaling any insects.

A good food source for very small frogs is aphids (commonly called greenfly or blackfly). These congregate in large numbers on the growing tips of many plants (especially cultivated ones). It is a simple matter to cut off a tip, complete with its ration of aphids, and place it in the terrarium.

Ants and termites can often be collected in large numbers. Though the former are usually rejected by most frog species (due to the formic acid taste), there are a few species which specialize in eating ants. Termites are taken eagerly by most species and they are a particularly nutritious item. If you have access to termite nests, you can simply chip a piece of the mound away at regular intervals, placing it, complete with the termites, in the terrarium. The nest will be quickly repaired by the termites left behind, leaving you with an almost continuous food supply.

Aquatic frogs and some carnivorous tadpoles require aquatic livefood. Various freshwater crustaceans, ranging from the tiny *Cyclops* and *Daphnia* to the relatively large freshwater shrimps and crayfish, can be netted or found by turning over rocks near the edges of streams, creeks etc. The larvae of many flying insects (mosquitos, mayflies, etc.) are aquatic and are also excellent food. When collecting aquatic livefoods, be careful not to introduce carnivorous larvae, such as those of dragonflies or water beetles, which will make short work of some of your tadpoles!

CULTURED LIVEFOODS

Although it would be ideal to be able to feed your animals collected livefood all the time, this is not always possible. Maybe you are short of time for collecting, or there is very little about (during the winter months in cooler areas). In such cases it is wise to have a standby supply of cultured livefoods. Today, there are many suppliers of various livefoods and, if you don't want to go to the trouble of breeding your own mealworms or crickets, for example, you can simply collect them or have a regular small supply of insects sent to your home. Some companies are even willing to supply, for example, a monthly order. However, many hobbyists choose to culture their own livefood, after having purchased the initial stock. The following is a brief guide to the more usual types of cultured livefood.

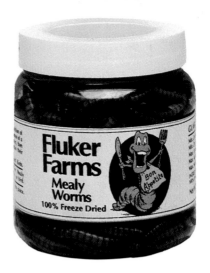

Mealworms: The larvae of the flour beetle (*Tenebrio molitor*), these creatures are probably the most well-known and oldest commercially produced livefoods for pet animals. They may be purchased from dealers in any quantity and are relatively easy to cultivate. Allow a few of the mealworms to pupate and metamorphose into adult beetles (these are brown and about 8 mm, .375 in long). The adult beetles are placed in a container with a close fitting but ventilated (gauze) lid, along with a 5 cm (2 in) layer of food mixture (bran plus crushed oats is ideal). Place a piece of burlap over the food mixture and put a couple of pieces of carrot or a similar vegetable on top to provide moisture. The beetles will soon mate and lay eggs in the food mixture. It takes about seven days for the eggs to hatch into tiny

mealworms, and these develop to full size in about 15 weeks. By starting a new culture each month, a regular supply of mealworms of all sizes will be available. For the best results, cultures should be kept at temperatures of 25–30°C (77–86°F).

Crickets: Crickets have become a popular cultured livefood only in recent years, but they are easy to breed and very nutritious. There are several species available, but the most commonly encountered are domestic species of the genus *Gryllus*. Cricket cultures can be obtained from cricket farms. They come in various sizes from .125 to 1 in, depending on what stage of the lifecycle they are in. This means that there is a size to suit most sizes of frog! Crickets are quite easy to breed in a ventilated plastic box, kept at a temperature of about 25°C (77°F). Feed the crickets on a mixture of bran and crushed oats, plus a little green food or raw root vegetable. A dish containing a piece of cotton soaked in water will double as a drinking fountain and a medium in which the insects can lay their eggs. The eggs will hatch in about 20 days and the young can be reared to various sizes.

Cockroaches: Cockroaches are common in many places, even in

Flies: There are literally thousands of species of flies, most of which are ideal food for frogs and toads. Fruitflies (*Drosophila* species) have long been used as experimental insects in laboratories. Due to the speed with which they reproduce, these little flies, about 2.5 mm (.125 in) in length, have been found to be ideal for genetic experiments. Consequently, their breeding has

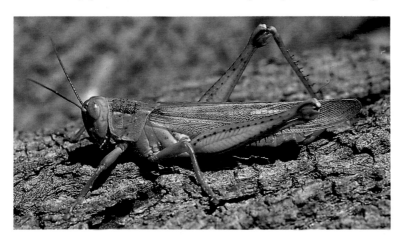

A colorful Australian grasshopper. Since grasshoppers and locusts are difficult to breed, it is a better idea to purchase or collect them occasionally rather than trying to create a steady supply.

inner cities. They are a versatile form of livefood for frogs and toads. Several species will breed if given similar conditions to crickets described above. The tiny nymphs make excellent food for smaller frogs.

Grasshoppers and Locusts: Good food value and larger than crickets, grasshoppers and locusts are somewhat more difficult to breed. Perhaps it is wise to just buy a few occasionally as a treat for your pets.

been taken to a fine art. Even vestigial winged specimens are bred in large numbers, and these are very useful for feeding to small frogs as you dispense with the problem of having the flies escaping to all corners of the house. Fruitfly cultures and instructions on how to proliferate them may be obtained from laboratories, biological suppliers, some pet shops, and even by mail order. Quantities of wild fruitflies can soon be collected if you place a box of banana skins or some rotten fruit in a remote corner of the garden. During the warmer parts of the year, this will be teeming with fruitflies in no time at all and they can be simply collected with a fine-mesh net.

Houseflies (*Musca* species) and lesser houseflies (*Fannia* species) are also suitable for small to medium-sized frogs, while the larger greenbottles (*Lucilia* species) and bluebottles (*Calliphora* species) are suitable for larger anurans. Most of these can be caught in a flytrap in the summer. A more convenient way of getting flies is to purchase maggots from a bait shop. The maggots themselves make a reasonable food for frogs, but do not use them in great numbers as they have a very tough skin and are hard to digest; just one or two occasionally is adequate. It is best to keep the maggots in containers of clean bran or sawdust and allow them to pupate. In a few days the adult flies will emerge. If you place a few pupae in a small plastic lunchbox with a fly-sized hole in the lid, the flies will escape singly and the whole box can be placed in the terrarium. Many frogs will soon learn of this food source and will patiently sit around the box waiting for flies to emerge.

Earthworms: Earthworms and brandlings can be purchased from bait suppliers or can be collected in the garden or elsewhere. They are excellent food for larger anurans or can be chopped into pieces for smaller ones. As pieces of earthworm continue to wriggle for some time after being chopped, they are accepted readily by many frog species. You can ensure a regular supply of earthworms by placing a pile of wet, dead leaves in a shady corner and covering it with a piece of sacking. If you spray the sacking with water regularly, earthworms will soon congregate among the decaying leaves, from where you can collect them at, say, weekly intervals. As one supply becomes exhausted, you can start again in another spot.

Whiteworms: These tiny worms (*Enchytraeus* species) can be purchased as cultures complete with instructions. They are a useful food for newly metamorphosed anurans or for very small species.

FOOD SUPPLEMENTS

In general, frogs which receive a wide selection of livefoods are unlikely to suffer from mineral or vitamin deficiencies. However, where a variety of insects is in short supply (such as during the winter when we have to make do with cultured foods such as mealworms or crickets over long periods), it is advisable to give a regular vitamin/mineral supplement, usually two or three times per week. Suitable vitamin/ mineral preparations may be obtained in liquid, powder or tablet form from drug stores, pet shops and veterinarians. Powders are most suitable for amphibians, as they can be dusted directly onto the livefood. The insects are placed in a small container and powder is dusted over them. A gentle shake will ensure that each insect has a film of powder over its

once, as excess food will soon pollute the water.

FEEDING STRATEGIES

Most anurans can be fed every other day; any more often may lead to refusal to feed. Feed only as much as will be taken in a few minutes. The correct amounts of food will have to be ascertained by experimentation. Most terrestrial species are initially attracted to

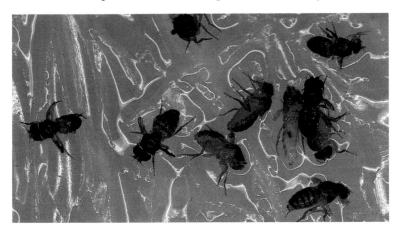

A group of wingless fruitflies, *Drosophila melanogaster*, congregating on an orange.

surface; the insects are then given to the frogs in the normal manner.

NON-LIVEFOODS

Xenopus, *Pipa*, and other aquatic frogs will take strips of meat or fish; some will even take trout pellets or other manufactured foods. Do not feed fatty meat but make it as lean as possible; the same goes for fish. Never provide more than the amphibians can eat at one sitting. A little bit quite often is better than too much at

their prey by its movement, so in most cases it is pointless giving dead food. However, some of the larger toads can be trained to take small pieces of meat by placing it in front of them and jiggling it with a very fine broom straw. The marine toad (*Bufo marinus*) is one of the few species which can be trained to voluntarily take immobile food, and some specimens have been known to tuck into a plate of steak and kidney as well as dog or cat food.

Hygiene and General Care

When confined in relatively small areas, as in the terrarium, the importance of hygiene cannot be underestimated. By hygiene we are not necessarily talking about soap and disinfectants but, in its most general sense, prevention of disease. Of course, cleanliness is a very important aspect of hygiene, but so is providing your terrarium inmates with optimum conditions for a life of contentment, devoid of stress. Stress in itself can be a factor which reduces an animal's normal resistance to disease, so we must ensure that our frogs' confinements are as comfortable as possible.

In general, frogs and toads are not very adaptable to surroundings which are alien to them. Just imagine what happens when we remove a frog from a cool, peaty, grassy meadow and place it in a tank containing chlorinated tapwater, at room temperature, in a house where the lights are left on until midnight. Common sense will tell you that this is just the situation to cause stress.

As discussed earlier, light intensity, photoperiod and temperature should be similar to those found in the frog's native habitat. Excessive chlorine, as well as excessive hardness, in some domestic water supplies can be dangerous to frog health. Use soft water where possible. If you can collect rainwater, this is ideal. Alternatively, leave tapwater to stand for at least 24 hours to allow free chlorine to disperse before it is used.

SELECTION OF SPECIMENS

One important aspect of hygiene is to ensure that your new animals are free of disease from the word go. This is especially important when you are introducing new animals to existing stock. Frogs which are captured in the wild are almost always healthy; those which had been ill would have been quickly eaten by predators. However, capture and confinement can induce stress, so try and make acclimation as comfortable as possible!

If you want to buy frogs from a pet shop, first impressions of the shop itself can be important. The manner in which animals are

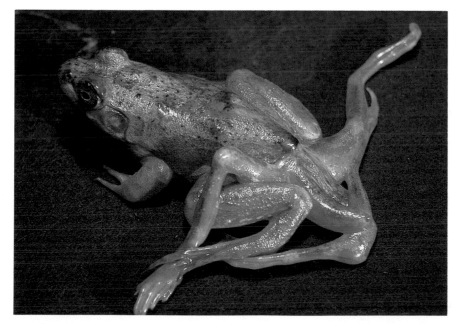

An eight-legged green frog, *Rana clamitans.* Genetic disasters like this sometimes occur; when they do, the best recourse is to end the animal's suffering with a quick, painless death.

25

commercially trapped, transported and confined for sale can be extremely stressful. Fortunately, legislation in many countries has now seen to it that animals, even "lowly" ones, get the best treatment possible. However, there are still some unscrupulous dealers who are out to make a quick buck. Never purchase animals from premises that are dirty, untidy and smelly, with overcrowded tanks. You will often see dead specimens mixed up with the live ones in such premises. A good pet shop owner is concerned with the welfare of every animal in his possession and will ensure that all are kept and displayed in the cleanest and most hygienic of conditions.

Individual specimens should be examined carefully before purchase; select those which are plump and have an unblemished skin. The eyes should be open and bright with correctly shaped pupils. Avoid specimens with sunken abdomens and exaggeration of the bones in the pelvic area; this is a sign of starvation, often brought on by some other disease. Specimens with injuries, sores or cysts on the skin should be discarded. Look for traces of fungus infection or red leg. Avoid specimens with obvious eye disorders. Specimens should be wary of the hand and should

attempt to hop away when touched. Do not accept specimens which show no fright, flight or fight.

HANDLING

Frogs and toads are not "pets" to be petted in the strict sense of the world. Most frogs and toads dislike being handled; additionally, a warm, sweaty hand is not only uncomfortable to a frog, but the salt content of the sweat can also be dangerous to it if you hold the delicate little creature for too long. Frogs and toads should be handled as infrequently as possible and then only for examination purposes. Many frogs unaccustomed to being handled will release the fluid contents of the cloaca upon being handled. This is a frog's reserve supply of body fluid and must be replaced. Ensure that a frog which has discharged its reserves has access to water as soon as possible. Frogs do not drink in the normal sense but absorb water through the skin.

One time when it will be necessary to handle a frog is when you are contemplating its purchase. Always wash the hands before handling and rinse them well in clear water, leaving them wet. A small frog can be gently cupped in the hands and examined by spreading the fingers. Large, robust specimens should be gripped gently but firmly around the waist, with their powerful hindlegs stretched out to prevent them from kicking. Aquatic frogs and tadpoles can be caught in a net made from soft material and examined without any need for handling, other than moving the net material away from the body.

Remember that many frogs and toads have powerful protective poisons which they release from glands in the skin. Some of these can be extremely dangerous if you get them in your eyes or mucus membranes. Therefore, always wash hands thoroughly after handling amphibians. Some species are also unable to tolerate the poisons of others, so don't keep more than one species together unless you are absolutely sure they are tolerant of each other.

TRANSPORT

Capture and transport are probably the most stressful times for frogs, so it is important that we make this process as easy as possible for them. Terrestrial frogs and toads can be transported in plastic "lunchboxes" with a number of holes drilled in the lid for ventilation purposes. To keep the frogs moist and to prevent them from being injured if the boxes are dropped or roughly handled, the boxes should be loosely packed with sphagnum moss. The animals should be transported as quickly as possible

The increasing popularity of herpetological specimens of all kinds has led to the availability of many new products designed specifically to benefit reptiles and amphibians. Photo courtesy of Coralife/ Energy Savers.

to their destination, via the shortest possible route. Transport boxes should never be left exposed to the sun's rays or left in a parked car in sunny weather. Conversely, tropical species must have some protection from chilling during cold weather, and in such cases it is wise to pack the transport boxes in some kind of an insulated container (a styrofoam box, for example).

QUARANTINE

If frogs are being introduced to existing stock, it is essential that they should first undergo a period of quarantine, to ensure that they are not sickening from some infectious disease which could be dangerous to all of your animals. Prepare a simple terrarium with a minimum of decorations but with the usual life-support systems and hiding places. This terrarium should preferably be kept in a separate room from the main stock. Install your new frogs in this quarantine terrarium and observe them carefully over the next 21 days. If the animals are still fit and healthy after the prescribed period, it should then be safe to introduce them to your other animals.

GENERAL HYGIENE

The hot, humid environments required by tropical species in particular are, unfortunately, also ideal conditions in which fungi, bacteria, etc., can grow. If we use sterile materials when setting up, and if we get the right balance between ventilation and humidity, then we will reduce the danger of bacterial proliferation to a minimum.

When handling objects in a particular terrarium, wash the hands before moving on to the next one. This is necessary even if there is no obvious sign of disease, and it will ensure that you are not the culprit in starting an epidemic among your charges. Terraria should be routinely cleaned out at regular intervals. Cleaning should consist only of scrubbing the terrarium and its furnishings with clean water. If you have had an outbreak of disease in a particular terrarium, isolate the sick animal(s) in a hospital terrarium in a separate room. Strip the terrarium and destroy plants, logs, etc., by burning. Rocks and gravel can be discarded or sterilized by boiling. The terrarium should be scrubbed out with a 10% solution of household bleach or with a veterinary povidone-iodine preparation, then thoroughly rinsed out with clean water.

HIBERNATION

Frogs from subtropical, montane or temperate climates hibernate during the colder parts of the year. They bury themselves in mud at the bottom of ponds or in deep terrestrial burrows, where they are safe from the frost. During hibernation, the basic metabolism is reduced dramatically—the animal is in a torpor and requires hardly any oxygen, let alone food. Although

warming, coupled with the extended photoperiod in the spring, that brings such frogs into breeding condition.

DISEASES AND TREATMENT

Kept in optimum environmental conditions and with good hygienic

Wood frog, *Rana sylvatica*. This species inhabits the forests and tundra of Alaska, Canada, and the northeastern United States.

hibernating species can be kept "awake" all year round in captivity, there is evidence to suggest that this may, in some species, reduce their life expectancy and also render them unlikely to breed. It is the period of hibernation and the slow

practices, anurans are remarkably resistant to diseases, and most cases of ill health can usually be blamed on some inadequacy in the care. Veterinary science with regard to amphibian diseases is still in its infancy and, unfortunately, cures for diseases

29

A pair of canyon tree frogs, *Hyla arenicolor*. When keeping more than one frog in the same terrarium, be sure that each one is getting enough to eat.

are often "hit and miss" affairs. However, there are a few veterinarians who devote themselves to the study of the more unusual types of pets, including frogs and toads. Your local veterinarian should be able to communicate with one or more of these experts if he is unsure himself. Some of the more common afflictions follow.

Nutritional Deficiencies: Usually caused by a lack of certain minerals or vitamins in the diet and common among frogs fed on a monotonous diet, of mealworms, for example. It is important to provide your frogs with as great a variety of foodstuffs as possible. A routine application of a powdered vitamin/mineral supplement to the food will prevent such deficiencies.

Mechanical Wounds: Open wounds or injuries to the skin are caused when frogs panic and attempt to escape from terraria. This usually occurs among newly captured specimens, which ideally should be left in peace until they are accustomed to their new surroundings. After this period of acclimation, such injuries will be less likely. Wounds are subject to bacterial infections which are potentially lethal, so treatment with an antibiotic may be necessary. Obtain advice from your veterinarian before applying any antiseptic preparations (some antiseptics which are quite safe for humans are lethal to amphibians).

Red-leg: This is the most infamous disease of captive frogs and is caused by the parasite *Aeromonas hydrophila*. Symptoms include the reddening of the skin, especially on the belly and the underside of the thighs. Infected animals become lethargic and apathetic. Infected animals should be immediately isolated. If caught in its early stages, red-leg may be treated by immersing the infected animal in a 2% solution of copper sulphate or potassium permanganate. The use of an antibiotic such as tetracycline may also help. Consult a veterinarian for advice about this lethal disease.

Spring Disease: This is a lethal disease which occurs among certain temperate species during the breeding season. It is caused by *Bacterium ranicida*. Symptoms include a discoloration of the skin, lethargy and a continuous "yawning." At present there seems to be no reliable treatment for this disease, though experimentation

with antibiotics may be worth a try. Consult your veterinarian.

Fungal Infections: These may be particularly troublesome in aquatic amphibians or in tadpoles. The disease is seen as areas of inflamed skin surrounded by whitish tissue. Untreated, these infections can prove fatal. If caught in its early stages, a fungus infection can be treated by immersing the animal in a 2% solution of malachite green or mercurochrome for five minutes, repeating after 24 hours if symptoms do not improve. If no improvement shows after three such treatments, a veterinarian should be consulted.

Colorado River toad, *Bufo alvarius*. **Members of this genus can be susceptible to skin diseases if their environment is not cleaned frequently.**

Breeding

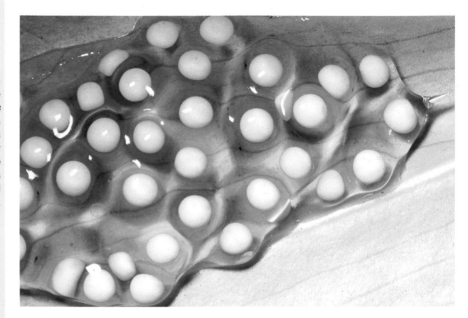

Egg mass from the red-eyed tree frog, *Agalychnis callidryas.* This species generally requires a large terrarium if it is to breed successfully.

Each individual species has its own unique breeding habits; however, a brief general summary on the captive breeding of frogs and toads will not go amiss. Most species require external stimuli to bring them into breeding condition. Temperate species, for example, usually breed in the spring, shortly after hibernation, and are affected by increases in temperature, photoperiod and intensity of light. Tropical species may be influenced by changes in humidity, either seasonal or coincidental. Some species can be persuaded to breed in captivity by injecting them with certain hormones. *Xenopus* species, for example, are regularly bred in laboratories after being injected with HCG (human chorionic gonadotrophin), a hormone which is produced by pregnant women. In fact, *Xenopus* frogs were once used in pregnancy tests for women before more convenient methods were discovered. Needless to say, if you contemplate using hormone injections to induce your frogs to breed, you must consult with a veterinarian or licensed animal technician.

With most species, the sexes should be kept separately until a breeding response is required. Hormone-treated *Xenopus* frogs will go into amplexus almost as soon as the pairs are introduced, and this will last for about 48 hours. It is best to place breeding *Xenopus* frogs into a spawning tank containing little other than the water, a heater, an aerator and a filter (ensure that the inlet to any filter is covered with fine mesh to prevent eggs or larvae from being sucked up). The eggs will fall to the bottom of the tank as they are being laid. A plastic grid, placed on stones just above the tank bottom, will allow the eggs to fall through and be protected from being eaten by the adults. After spawning, the adults can be moved back to their permanent tanks and the spawning tank can also be used as a rearing tank. The best temperature for hatching and rearing is 18–22°C (65–72°F), but the eggs will tolerate temperatures as low as 15°C (59°F) or as high as 25°C (77°F).

Dead eggs (which turn opaque white) and/or larvae should be removed with a pipette as soon as they arc seen. For the first 72 hours after hatching the tadpoles will not require feeding, as they will be absorbing the contents of

A string of Common European toad, *Bufo bufo*, eggs. Members of this genus lay thousands of eggs, which are often preyed upon by newts.

the yolk sac. As soon as they start to swim actively, they will feed. Grass or nettle powder may be used as a basic food; to this is added very small amounts (about 5% each) of powdered, dried yeast, egg powder, and a vitamin/mineral preparation. These ingredients are thoroughly mixed together and water is added to make a paste. A pinch added to the rearing tank daily is adequate at first, with this amount being increased slightly every few days as the larvae grow. As soon as the limbs are fairly well developed, one can start feeding the metamorphosing larvae on mosquito larvae, *Cyclops*, *Daphnia*, and chopped tubifex or whiteworm (do not overfeed with the chopped food).

Seasonal breeders which spawn in large bodies of water can be given similar treatment to *Xenopus* species in the early stages. Water temperature will, of course, depend on the native habitat of the species in question. For temperate species, pairs are introduced in the spring, after one has begun to gradually increase temperature and photoperiod. These increases should continue until a maximum of 20°C (68°F) and a 15-hour period of "daylight" has

been reached. Amphibious species which live on land after metamorphosis should be given facilities to leave the water as soon as they are ready. This can be done by rearing them in an aqua-terrarium with a sloping "bank." Alternatively, they may be reared in shallow water in which large flat stones are placed so that they just break the water surface.

When breeding anurans which produce great numbers of offspring, it will be necessary to cull some of the tadpoles off in order to prevent overcrowding. As the tadpoles grow, weed out the smaller specimens and dispose of them; native specimens can be released in a suitable pond but do *not* release exotic specimens which could be a future ecological hazard. It is much better to rear a small number of fit, healthy specimens than to have numerous weaklings.

Yosemite toad, *Bufo canorus*.

A Selection of Species

With over 3500 species, it is impossible to list more than a token sample of the frogs and toads of the world in a small volume such as this. However, by selecting a few examples of the more popular species kept as pets, the author hopes to whet the appetite of those eager to delve further into the infinite variety of these fascinating creatures.

In the following accounts, the lengths given are from snout to vent and are the maximum size you would expect an adult of that particular species to grow. In most cases specimens are likely to mature at lengths somewhat shorter than those given.

THE AQUATIC PIPIDS

The Pipidae is a relatively small family of highly aquatic anurans with interesting lifestyle and breeding habits. As such, they are very popular with the aquarium keeper who likes to keep something "different." The Pipidae is divided into two subfamilies: the Pipinae, with a single genus and

Surinam toad, *Pipa pipa*. This rough-and-tumble species has been known to decimate its surroundings; therefore, only hardy waterplants should be used in the terrarium.

seven species inhabiting tropical America, and the Xenopodinae, with three genera and 19 species inhabiting parts of Africa south of the Sahara.

Surinam Toad
Pipa pipa

This must be one of the most bizarre-looking and interesting of all anurans and, as such, is a very popular animal with terrarium keepers. This species is one of about seven in the subfamily Pipinae, all of which are native to the northern parts of South America, one reaching as far north as Panama. *Pipa pipa* is found in slow-moving watercourses from Colombia to Bolivia, Peru and Ecuador and from the Guianas to parts of Brazil, Venezuela and Trinidad.

The Surinam toad has a flattened body and a pointed snout. Its arms are relatively small, and the unwebbed fingers are furnished at the tips with very sensitive, star-like appendages used to locate food items in murky waters. The legs are large and powerful and the huge feet are provided with long, completely webbed toes. The eyes are relatively small and, as in all pipids, are situated on top of the head. The color is a rather drab mixture of grays and browns on top and off-white underneath.

This species is nocturnal and

Female *Pipa carvalhoi* giving birth to live young (the spike on her back).

spends most of the day quietly laying on the substrate, preferably in a dark spot. It has the appearance of being a rather sluggish creature but can move remarkably fast when it comes up for air or when feeding.

A pair may be kept in an aquarium with a capacity of not less than 150 liters (approximately 35 gallons) and a water depth of not less than 30 cm (12 in). Substrate should consist of a rather coarse gravel and only robust plants, if any, should be used. For most of the year, the temperature can be maintained at around 26°C (79°F). An aquarium filter and some kind of recirculatory system is considered essential for these anurans. A jugful of water should be exchanged each day. Feed the toads on live fishes (guppies for example), strips of lean meat (beef, chicken or ox heart), and earthworms.

The most interesting aspect of the Surinam toad is its unusual

breeding habits. In the wild state, the animals are induced to breed by the rainy season which follows a period of drought. In captivity the situation can be simulated by slowly reducing the water level until it is just 15 cm (6 in) in depth. Then, one day the water is suddenly returned to not less than 30 cm (12 in) in depth, with a reduction in temperature to about 20°C (68°F), allowed to return slowly to 26°C (79°F) over a period of 24 hours. This should induce the toads to breed. First the male will emit his comical, metallic sounding "click-click-click," often for several hours,

before grasping the female around the hips. While in amplexus, the pair performs a series of "somersaults," and each time the water surface is reached (in an upside-down position) the female releases a small number of eggs (usually three to six) through her long ovipositor. The eggs are fertilized by the male, who then guides them onto the female's back which, by this time, will have become quite spongy. Some of the eggs may fall to the substrate, but these will be wasted and should preferably be removed with a pipette (after spawning is over). After performing several

Surinam toad, *Pipa pipa*. Members of this species almost never leave the water.

somersaults, often over a period of several hours, and having laid 40–100 eggs, the pair will separate. The eggs will adhere to the female's back, and in the next 24 hours the skin will begin to swell around the eggs until each one has its own individual chamber. Complete development of the larva and metamorphosis occurs in each of these little nursery chambers, and in 12–20 weeks perfectly formed little Surinam toads will emerge. These should be removed to a rearing tank and raised on tiny aquatic vertebrate,

African Clawed Frog
Xenopus laevis

A member of the family Pipidae, subfamily Xenopodinae, this is one of the most well known and popular of the aquatic frogs, used both in laboratories and as a pet. It was this species which was used in pioneer pregnancy testing in women; the chorionic hormone produced by a pregnant woman would cause the frogs to ovulate. The clawed frog reaches about 12.5 cm (5 in) in length and is powerfully built, with strong hindlegs and webbed toes well adapted for swimming. The toes are armed with sharp "claws" which give the animal its common name. As this is an unusual feature in anurans, the scientific name *Xenopus*, derived from the Greek,

means literally "strange foot."

The clawed frog has a very smooth, slippery skin, making it difficult to hold in the hand; it is thus normally handled with a net. The normal color is gray to brown on the dorsal surface, marbled with darker shades. The underside is creamy white. Color mutations, including albinos, "goldens," and pieds, are available. The small eyes are set on top of the head. Females are somewhat larger than the males and the former can be recognized by the three lobes or appendages arranged around the cloaca.

The native habitat of the clawed frog is in slow-moving streams and ponds in savannah regions of eastern and southern Africa. During the dry seasons the adults are able to estivate in the thick muddy substrate of the water courses. New rains and flooding encourage breeding. Although it prefers to remain aquatic, the clawed frog is able to move over land to new water courses during wet weather.

In captivity, a pair of clawed frogs can be comfortably housed in an aquarium 60 cm long by 30 cm deep by 40 cm wide (24 x 12 x 16 in). Provide a gravel substrate and (preferably) a mechanical filter. Maintain at a temperature of 22–27°C (71–80°F). The water should be 15–20 cm (6–8 in) deep, or just deep enough for the frogs to break the surface with the snout while the toes are touching the substrate. Floating plants and rocks may be added for decoration. Plants in the substrate will usually be uprooted by the frogs in the search for food unless you have very well-established plants in a very large container. *Xenopus* frogs can be kept in outdoor pools in sub-tropical to tropical climates or even in milder temperate areas, but care should be taken to prevent escape of this species into the wild, as it can have a devastating effect on local ecology. It has become a successful colonist in southern California and is, in fact, prohibited in parts of the western USA for this very reason.

This species may be fed on small strips of lean, raw meat, especially beefsteak, ox heart, or chicken. Earthworms are taken readily as well as the more common invertebrate foods. When meat must be given over long periods, a vitamin/mineral supplement should be added to it. Laboratory stock are often fed on specially formulated pellets (similar to trout pellets, which are also acceptable should *Xenopus* pellets not be available). Uneaten food must be removed from the water before it putrefies. It is

advisable to change a jugful (about 1 liter or 2 pints) of the tank water every day and to give the tank a complete cleaning and water change every three months.

Although *Xenopus laevis* is the most common clawed frog in captivity, there are 13 other species from various parts of Africa listed in Frost. Other species in the genus—of which *X. muelleri* (9 cm, 3.75 in, from central and southern Africa) is probably the most frequently available—require similar care.

Dwarf Clawed Frog
Hymenochirus boettgeri

In the same subfamily as *Xenopus*, there are four described species of *Hymenochirus*, of which *H. boettgeri* is the best known. Hailing from the rainforest areas of central and western Africa, this little frog reaches a maximum length of 3.5 cm (1.5 in). The skin is relatively rough, the body is dorso-ventrally flattened, and the head is small with a pointed snout; there are no eyelids. The dorsal surface is gray-brown with marbling of a darker color; underside is a uniform grayish to yellowish white. The toes and

the male grasps the female around the waist and both then rise to the surface, turning over onto their backs as they do so. The male pumps at the female, who lays about ten to 20 tiny eggs at a time, and these are simultaneously fertilized by the male sperm. The

Dwarf African clawed frog, *Hymenochirus boettgeri*. In the wild, this species is found in still and slow-moving waters.

fingers are webbed.

This almost totally aquatic species can be kept in similar conditions to *Xenopus* species, although a smaller tank may be used and the water should be shallower and the temperature maintained at about 23°C. The dwarf clawed frog should also be fed on a similar diet, although the respective food items should be relatively smaller. *H. boettgeri* can be induced to breed by raising the ambient temperature by 4–5°C (8–10°F) to about 27–28°C (80–82°F). Mating behavior shows many similarities to that of *Pipa*;

pair sink to the substrate and the process is repeated until as many as 1000 eggs are laid and fertilized. Eggs may be removed with a pipette and placed in a container of clean aerated water maintained at about 25°C (77°F). They will hatch in about three days, and in another three days the larvae will become free-swimming and seek food. The larvae of *Hymenochirus* are carnivorous and start feeding on tiny microorganisms (infusoria or a jarful of stagnant pond water should be added to the rearing tank at regular intervals—just beware

that no tadpole predators are introduced!), but as they grow they will take *Cyclops*, *Daphnia*, and finely chopped tubifex worms.

THE "WARTY" BUFONID TOADS

The typical toad with its dry, warty skin is a member of the family Bufonidae. This is one of the largest of the anuran families, containing some 25 genera and over 330 species found in most parts of the world with the exception of Australasia, Madagascar and most oceanic islands, although artificial introductions have seen toads successfully colonize even some of these habitats. The genus *Bufo* alone contains over 200 species, most of which are typically "toadlike," and many are extremely difficult to distinguish from each other.

Common European Toad
Bufo bufo

The original "toad," first scientifically described by Linnaeus as *Rana bufo*, is the common European toad, now scientifically known as *Bufo bufo*. Found in suitable habitats in most of Europe and extending far into Asia, this species is a typical

41

example of what the average person expects a toad to to look like. Growing to about 10 cm (4 in) in the northern and 15 cm (6 in) in the southern part of its range, the toad has a plump, robust body, relatively short arms and legs, and large golden eyes with horizontal pupils. The skin is dry to the touch and is covered with numerous "warts," which are in fact poison glands—very effective in protecting toads from predators. The upperside is a mottled mixture of browns or grays and may take on a reddish or yellowish tinge, to resemble the color of the earth in which the toad lives. The underside is off-white mottled with dark gray to brown.

Like most toads, this species spends the greater part of the year on dry land, holing up under a rock or log during the day and setting forth to forage for invertebrates at night. It normally walks but is capable of bursts of speed with rapid hops, usually when alarmed. Most toads make very satisfying and endearing "pets," quickly settling into terrarium life, and they are relatively intelligent—at least in anuran circles. This species can be kept in an unheated terrarium with a few potted plants and hiding places such as stone caves, hollow logs, or broken crocks. Substrate can consist of a mixture of peat, sand, and leaf litter, kept very slightly damp. Outside the breeding season, a small water dish is adequate for the toads to soak themselves occasionally.

The temperature should preferably be kept below 22°C (72°F) and may be allowed to reduce itself to natural levels at night in temperate areas. Food consists of a variety of invertebrates, and, as toads are somewhat gluttonous, the meals should be regulated to prevent the onset of obesity. A winter hibernation period of two to three months at 4–5°C (39–41°F) will help bring the toads into spring breeding condition. In the wild, this species breeds in early spring. The males assemble first at suitable ponds, the females arriving a few days later. Males often outnumber the females by as much as five to one, and this is believed to be a natural breeding strategy which ensures that each female receives attention from a healthy, fertile male. The male grasps the female firmly around the thoracic region, just behind her arms, and the pair move about as the female lays a double "string" of eggs which may be wound around waterplants or other submerged objects such as bicycle frames or bedsteads. After spawning, the females leave the water immediately to spend another year on the land; the males may stay in the water for a few

"Like most toads, this species spends the greater part of the year on dry land, holing up under a rock or log during the day and setting forth to forage for invertebrates at night."

more days, perhaps in the hope of getting another female. The toad eggs hatch in a few days and the larvae develop into tiny toads by late summer. The newly metamorphosed toadlets leave the water in great numbers as soon as suitable weather arrives. Humid or rainy weather will often result in the "plague" of toads, which one often hears about.

B. bufo is unlikely to breed in the confines of an indoor terrarium and is more likely to do so in the relatively large pond of a cool greenhouse or an outdoor enclosure. Another European species, the green toad, *Bufo viridis*, is a very colorful species and thus popular with terrarium keepers. Its cream to brown background color is marked with vivid olive to grass green patches. Its care is similar to that of the common toad, though summer heating to around 26°C (79°F) is recommended.

American Toad
Bufo americanus

North America boasts at least 18 species of toads in the genus *Bufo*, but the so-called American toad, *B. americanus*, is the one most familiar to inhabitants of Eastern USA. Superficially similar to *B. bufo* in appearance, this species grows to 11 cm (4.5 in) in length. There are three well-defined subspecies, and the colors

Albino American toad, *Bufo americanus*. Most members of this genus adapt well to captivity and may even "beg" for food.

range from brown to brick red above, patterned with lighter colors. There is sometimes a light vertebral stripe.

It is found in the eastern part of North America from central Canada through to the southern states (but not reaching the Gulf Coast, where it is replaced by the southern toad, *B. terrestris*). Its habits and breeding requirements are very similar to the European toad and it requires similar accommodation and care. Other North American toads requiring similar care include the western toad, *B. boreas*; Great Plains toad, *B. cognatus*; Canadian toad, *B.*

hemiophrys; and the particularly common and wide-ranging Woodhouse's toad, *B. woodhousei*.

Giant, Marine or Cane Toad
Bufo marinus

This species warrants a special mention. It is typically toadlike with a dry warty skin and extremely large parotid glands. Its poison is particularly virulent, and it grows to 25 cm (10 in) in length! Although most people regard it as ugly and noxious, frog lovers treat it as a prized pet. Indeed, this species can get to being as near to

Western toad, *Bufo boreas*. This species spawns in somewhat saline inland lakes; therefore, it may be able to tolerate salt water.

a pet as any amphibian could. It becomes tame, trusting and even gets to recognize its owner. It is one of the few species which will take inanimate food, and some fanciers delight in fattening up their specimens with dog or catfood or even raw steak!

This toad is usually a uniform gray-brown to red-brown with a lighter underside. Juvenile specimens may be substantially and often quite prettily marked with lighter colors, but these are lost as the toad grows. The enormous parotid glands, extending down the sides of the body from just behind the eyes, release a milky fluid when the toad is roughly handled. This fluid is highly toxic, will burn the eyes and mucus membranes, and will irritate the skin of some people. The hands should always be carefully washed after handling any amphibian but especially this one. A dog or cat which tries to savage a giant toad can even die from the effects of the poison, so don't mix your toads with your other pets!

The natural range of the giant toad is Central America and northern South America. It extends slightly into the USA in southern Texas, and it has become feral in Florida. The predatory habits of this species have, in the past, led to its introduction in many other parts of the world as a controller of

agricultural pests. In some areas it has colonized so successfully that it has become a pest in its own right, threatening native fauna with displacement and poisoning domestic animals. In Australia, where it was introduced from Hawaii (where it had been introduced in 1932) in 1935 to combat the sugar cane pest, it is now considered to be a serious threat to many native amphibians and reptiles. It is also a prohibited animal in several states of the USA.

This toad is primarily nocturnal, coming out at night to hunt. During dry periods it will estivate. The toads are commonly attracted to street or porch lights at night, where they will congregate in groups, waiting to snap up any unfortunate insects when they fall to the ground. It is a very easy captive and can be kept in a large terrarium or even given the run of

Giant toad, *Bufo marinus*. This species is primarily nocturnal, hiding by day and hunting invertebrates at night.

the house. It likes a water bath in which it will soak in hot weather. Temperatures up to 28°C (82°F) during the day and reduced to about 20°C (68°F) at night are suitable. Feed on a variety of larger invertebrates (grasshoppers, earthworms, beetles, moths) and small vertebrates (pink mice, small fish, etc.). Can be trained to take lean meat, dogfood, etc., from the fingers. This species is unlikely to breed in a small terrarium but will do so in a large heated pool. Like *Xenopus* species, it can be induced to breed with hormone injections and has in the past been used for pregnancy tests in some parts of the world.

THE SLIPPERY RANID FROGS

The family Ranidae contains what can be described as the typical frogs, most of which have a smooth, slippery skin and powerful hindlimbs for jumping. In his system of classification, Linnaeus placed all frogs (and toads) known at the time in the genus *Rana*, but since then, this family has been revised many

Common European grass frog, *Rana temporaria*. Unfortunately, several *Rana* species are sought-after for their legs, which are often considered a delicacy.

times and has grown to include three subfamilies, about 40 genera, and over 600 species found on every continent except Antarctica. Included in this family is the world's largest frog, the goliath frog, *Conraua goliath*, from West Africa, which grows to 40 cm (16 in) in length.

Common European Grass Frog
Rana temporaria

This was probably the very first frog to get a scientific name (in 1758), but it is now one of 270 more species in the same genus. *R. temporaria* is found throughout central and northern Europe as far north as the Arctic Circle and east to the Ural Mountains. All ranid frogs are "typically froglike" with a smooth, slippery skin and long powerful hindlegs, which makes them excellent swimmers and leapers. The common European grass frog is a member of the "brown frog" (as opposed to the "green frog") complex. It reaches about 10 cm (4 in) in length, is highly variable in color, and ranges through shades of brown, olive, gray, yellowish or reddish above with darker markings below. A prominent black or dark brown patch from the rear of the eye to the corner of the mouth and including the eardrum is a trademark of the species. The underside is off-white with darker marbling.

This species is terrestrial for most of the year, where it inhabits damp, grassy meadows, woodland, and gardens but rarely wanders far from permanent water. It is primarily nocturnal but may be active during the day in secluded areas. This species is probably best suited to an outdoor enclosure, though it may be kept in an unheated terrarium (temperatures below 20°C, 68°F) for short periods for closer observation. Feed on a variety of small invertebrates. Unlikely to breed in a small aquarium, with outdoor ponds preferred; however, collected spawn can easily be reared to metamorphosis in an aqua-terrarium. Other European "brown frogs" requiring similar captive care include the moor frog, *R. arvalis*; the agile frog, *R. dalmatina*; the stream frog, *R. graeca*; and the Iberian frog, *R. iberica*. Southern species require slightly higher temperatures.

Moor frog, *Rana arvalis*, another European species.

Edible Frog
Rana esculenta

The edible frog is a member of the "green frog" complex of European ranids. These are much more aquatic than their brown counterparts; their terrestrial excursions are confined to sunning themselves on the banks but quickly returning to water if disturbed. Growing to about 13 cm (5 in) in length, this robust species may be predominantly green to brownish, with darker markings. There may be a light dorsal stripe. The males have paired vocal sacs which protrude at the corners of the mouth during bouts of loud croaking. This species is found throughout central Europe and into Italy, but it is absent from Iberia and the Balkans.

Captive specimens require a large aqua-terrarium with more water than land area. The water should be not less than 25 cm (10 in) deep. It is perhaps better suited

to an outdoor enclosure with a deep pool. It will feed on a variety of invertebrates which it can catch both above or below the water surface. Summer temperatures can reach 25°C (77°F) during the day, with a reduction at night. Hibernation for about three months at 4–5°C (39–41°F).

generally accepted that *R. esculenta* is a sort of fertile hybrid of the other two species and contains sets of chromosomes from both.

Northern Leopard Frog
Rana pipiens
In North America, the genus

One of the leopard frogs. *Rana pipiens* is actually a complex of approximately a dozen similar species found from southern Canada to Mexico.

Unlikely to breed in indoor terraria, but females may lay up to 10,000 eggs in deeper outdoor pools. The smaller (9 cm, 3.5 in) pool frog, *R. lessonae*, and the larger (15 cm, 6 in) marsh frog, *R. ridibunda*, are similar apart from size and require similar care. All three species occur in Europe, and their ranges overlap considerably in some areas. Hybridization occurs, frequently causing many taxonomic problems. It is now

Rana is well represented, with members of the leopard frog complex being the most abundant. The northern leopard frog is the common frog of the southern half of Canada and the northern half of the USA with the exception of the western coastal areas. Reaching 8 cm (3.25 in) in length, it is a slender greenish to brownish frog with large, dark spots, usually edged with gray or white. There is a light stripe along the upper jawline. The six to ten other leopard frog species in Canada, USA, and Mexico are all very similar and (still) pose enormous problems to taxonomists. All have similar habits, however, and may be treated similarly in captivity. They are found in a variety of habitats, from freshwater lakes with thick vegetation to brackish marshland, and from sea level to montane meadow. Mainly found in or near water, where it takes cover when threatened. Requires a large aqua-terrarium with roughly half land and half water areas, the latter to a depth of at least 15 cm (6 in). Aquatic and terrestrial plants may be used for decoration. Summer temperature to 25°C (77°F), reduced to around 15°C (59°F) at night. Leopard frogs should be fed

on a variety of small invertebrates. *R. pipiens* is one of easiest ranid frogs to breed in captivity; it can be induced to spawn after a winter rest period by increasing temperature and photoperiod. This species is frequently used as an experimental laboratory animal.

Apart from the leopard frogs, there are a number of other North American ranids which require similar husbandry. These include the crawfish frog, *R. areolata*; the green frog, *R. clamitans*; and the wood frog, *R. sylvatica*. Similar, but with a more aquatic habitat, are the pig frog, *R. grylio*; the river frog, *R. heckscheri*; and the carpenter frog, *R. virgatipes*.

Bullfrog
Rana catesbeiana
The famous American bullfrog

Bullfrog, *Rana catesbeiana*. This very aquatic species is found in lakes, ponds, marshes, and small rivers.

is a large species reaching 20 cm (8 in) in length. It is usually mottled greenish to brownish, and the powerful hindlimbs are usually banded in dark and light brown. The tympanum, especially in the male, is very prominent. It has a single vocal sac beneath the chin, with which it is able to emit its deep groaning "jug o' rum" call. Its natural range is eastern and central USA, but in attempts to commercially harvest frogs' legs it has been successfully introduced to the West Coast and to other parts of the world, including parts of northern Italy. It is very aquatic in its habits and prefers large, deep but well vegetated ponds, lakes, rivers, and marshes. It is active both by day and at night but its call is usually emitted at dusk or during the hours of darkness.

It must have a very large aqua-terrarium with more water than land and a water depth of at least 45 cm (18 in). It should preferably be kept in a greenhouse or outdoor enclosure with a deep pool, where it is much more likely to breed. Summer temperatures to 26°C (79°F) are required, with a slight reduction at night. Hibernation for two to three months at 4–5°C (39–41°F). It may be fed on a variety of large invertebrates and small vertebrates. In the wild, large specimens are known to eat small birds and snakes, though aquatic insects, crayfish and small fish seem to be its staple diet. The tadpoles grow very large and may pass the winter in the larval stage.

African Bullfrog
Pyxicephalus adspersus

This member of the family Ranidae is one of only two species in its genus. In recent times this large (up to 20 cm, 8 in), gluttonous frog has become very popular with the terrarium keeper; fortunately, it is a very common frog over much of Africa south of the equator. In the more arid areas it estivates for much of the year, becoming sexually active at the onset of sudden rains, and it is able to complete its metamorphosis in temporary waters in relatively short periods. The metamorphosed frogs are cannibalistic and will think nothing of swallowing their smaller brothers and sisters. The African bullfrog is primarily green above and its back is ornamented with a number of raised longitudinal ridges. Underneath, it is yellowish white, becoming bright yellow to orange on the throat, under the forelimbs and in the groin. It has large canine-like projections in the lower jaw, and large specimens are capable of giving a vicious bite.

In spite of its size, this species will do well in a relatively small terrarium. It should be provided with a fairly deep substrate, consisting of a mixture of gravel and leaf litter, in which it will bury itself up to its neck, ready to lunge at any passing food item. It can take a variety of large invertebrates, including earthworms, cockroaches, moths, and beetles as well as young mice. A large adult specimen is capable of swallowing a full-grown mouse, though these should not be given too often or the frog will become too fat and may die prematurely. It should be provided with a fairly large water bath in which it will frequently bathe. Maintain at a temperature of about 25–28°C

"The metamorphosed frogs are cannibalistic and will think nothing of swallowing their smaller brothers and sisters."

(77–82°F), reduced to room temperature at night. Do not keep with smaller frogs even of its own species unless you want them to disappear!

This species is unlikely to breed in the smaller terrarium, though it may breed in a deep, heated pond in a greenhouse after a simulated "dry season" followed by "heavy rainfall." It is said that the males stay in the water near the spawn, defending both this and the hatchling tadpoles until they become free swimming.

THE HYLID TREE DWELLERS

The family Hylidae contains four subfamilies and some 37 genera. Many of those species commonly known as tree frogs are included, but by no means are all of the 640 species arboreal, some being surface dwellers or even burrowers. Many of the tree frogs make ideal terrarium inmates. There is room here only to suggest a few of the more well known species.

Spring Peeper
Hyla crucifer

Hyla is the largest genus in the family, with over 250 species found in Eurasia, northern Africa and the Americas. One of the best known North American species is the spring peeper, which occurs throughout the eastern half of the

continent, from central Canada down to the Gulf Coast. In its range, the high-pitched pipping call of the male frog is recognized as one of the first signs of spring. It is a tiny frog, barely reaching 3.5 cm (1.375 in) in length. It may be reddish, grayish or dark brown in color, characterized by a darker X-shaped marking on the back. Like most tree frogs, this little fellow has large, flat, sucker-like toe pads to enable it to get a grip on the foliage of trees and shrubs often near or overhanging water.

It requires a small but tall terrarium with a potted shrub and a pool of water in the base. Supplementary heating is unnecessary unless the southern subspecies is kept in northern areas. Feed on very small invertebrates including juvenile crickets, fruitflies, lesser houseflies and mosquitoes (place collected mosquito larvae in the terrarium pool and allow to metamorphose into adults, but be sure that the terrarium ventilating mesh is of a small enough gauge to prevent mosquitoes from escaping into the house).

Green Tree Frog
Hyla cinerea

Growing to 5 cm (2 in) in length, this little frog is found in southern and southeastern USA. It it predominantly green above, with a dark-edged, broad white stripe extending along the upper lip and about halfway along the body. Mainly nocturnal, it lives in foliage near permanent water, often resting on the underside of large leaves.

It requires a tall terrarium with large-leaved plants and a climbing

Green tree frog, *Hyla cinerea*. This species has been successfully bred in captivity.

log. Should be kept fairly humid with good ventilation. The daytime temperature can reach 27°C (81°F), reduced at night to about 20°C (68°F). Feed on various species of flies, crickets, moths, and other small to medium-sized vertebrates. A period of reduced temperature at about 10°C (50°F) for a couple of months will

gray tree frogs, *H. versicolor* and *H. chrysoscelis*; and the squirrel tree frog, *H. squirella*.

European Tree Frog
Hyla arborea

A plump little frog with a smooth skin, the European tree frog is usually bright green on the back with a dark stripe running

One of the gray tree frogs, *Hyla versicolor*. This species is relatively common in the eastern United States.

simulate hibernation and increase chances of breeding; however, this is more likely to be successful in a greenhouse with a suitable pond rather than in the confines of a relatively small terrarium. Other North American species with similar requirements are the Pacific tree frog, *H. regilla*; the

from the eye and down the side of the body, though it can change quite dramatically to brown or yellowish depending on its situation and mood. Reaching 5 cm (2 in) in total length, it is found in most of Europe except for the north and extends into Asia as far as the Caspian Sea. It requires similar husbandry to *H. cinerea*, as do two closely related species: the stripeless tree frog, *H. meridionalis*, from southern Europe and N. Africa; and the Japanese tree frog, *H. japonica*, from eastern Asia.

Red-eyed Tree Frog
Agalychnis callidryas

Within the family Hylidae but in the subfamily Pelomedusidae there are some quite bizarre and attractive species. The red-eyed tree frog of Central America is one of the most spectacular of all frogs. Reaching 7.5 cm (3 in) in length, it has a slender body and extraordinarily thin limbs. It is leaf green on the back, often sprinkled with a few white spots. The flanks are vertically banded in sky-blue and cream; the limbs are green

above and blue below, while the feet and padded toes are a bright orange-red. Probably its most prominent feature is the pair of large, spectacular, crimson red eyes with vertical pupils.

This is a strictly arboreal and nocturnal frog of the tropical rainforest. It is a rather delicate captive and should be considered only by experienced fanciers. It should be kept in a tall, well-ventilated terrarium with high humidity, preferably accomplished with moving water (an airlift waterfall or drip system) or with regular mist spraying. Large-leaved plants such as *Philodendron* or *Monstera* species should be provided. Maintain at a temperature of 25–28°C (77–82°F), reduced to 20°C (68°F at night). Feed on a variety of

A pair of red-eyed tree frogs, *Agalychnis callidryas*. Members of this species typically move with a stealthy, stalking action, jumping only when necessary.

invertebrates, especially flies and moths. This species breeds in the foliage canopy, and eggs are laid on leaves overhanging a pool or stream. The larvae drop into the water as they hatch a few days later. These develop in the normal way, leaving the water as fully developed little tree frogs a few weeks later. Require a large terrarium with pool if captive breeding is to be accomplished.

White's Tree Frog
Litoria caerulea

Members of the genus *Litoria* were formerly included within *Hyla*, but along with other Australian and New Guinea species were relegated to their own subfamily (Pelodryadinae) in 1977 and received a new generic name. White's tree frog is one of the most endearing of the 100 or so species of *Litoria*, as it seems to become tame and trusting from the day it is taken into captivity. Reaching a length of 10 cm (4 in), it is one of the larger members of the subfamily. It is also a very robust species which often gives the impression of being "overweight," due to its plumpness and the folds of flesh seen on older specimens. It has large finger and toe pads. The color is predominantly bluish-green (all-blue specimens occasionally turn up), sometimes with a few small but vivid white spots scattered over the back. Its underside is usually a creamy or yellowish white.

It occurs in the eastern and northern parts of Australia and in southern New Guinea, where it is

frequently found near human habitations, often seeking out the dampness associated with domestic water tanks, dams and cisterns. It is mainly nocturnal and has a deep, throaty croak. In captivity it should be provided with a large, tall terrarium with robust plants and solid branches on which it can climb. Keep the humidity moderate, with good ventilation and daytime temperatures to 30°C (86°F), but reduced to around 20°C (68°F) at night. Feed on a variety of larger invertebrates, including crickets, locusts, cockroaches, beetles, and moths. Requires a deep (not less than 30 cm, 12 in) pool if breeding is contemplated. May be brought into breeding condition by a severe increase in humidity over a period of several days.

THE SPADEFOOTS OR PELOBATIDS

The family Pelobatidae contains two subfamilies, nine genera, and about 74 species. The best known members of the family are the North American and European spadefoots of the genera *Scaphiopus* and *Pelobates* in the subfamily Pelobatinae. These frogs are characterized by having a prominent, flattened, sharp-edged "spade" on the heel of the foot. These are, in fact, modified metatarsal tubercles which enable the amphibian to quickly bury

itself in the (usually) sandy substrate in which it lives. Although often referred to as toads, the spadefoots are easily distinguished from the bufonids, as they have a relatively smooth skin.

Couch's Spadefoot Toad
Scaphiopus couchi

Reaching 9 cm (3.5 in) in length, this is a plump little toad with a relatively long, sickle-shaped spade on each foot. The fairly smooth skin has many tiny, light-colored tubercles. The color is bright greenish yellow to brown, with darker marbling. The underside is predominantly off-white. It occurs from southeastern California through to southwestern Oklahoma and south into Mexico, where it prefers short grass prairie. It is quite tolerant of arid conditions but will estivate in a deep burrow during excessively dry periods. In more humid periods it emerges each night to

Couch's spadefoot, *Scaphiopus couchi*. Members of this species have been known to burrow their way out of outdoor enclosures.

hunt for its insect prey, burrowing again before it is endangered by the harsh rays of the daytime sun.

It requires a terrarium with a deep, loose substrate (coarse sand). Provide a dish of water, but the substrate itself may be kept reasonably dry. The daytime air temperature can be as high as 30°C (86°F) and humidity can be low. Reduce temperature at night to around 20°C (58°F). Reduce temperature in winter to 10°C (50°F) for a couple of months of simulated hibernation. In the wild, breeding occurs after heavy rain and flash-flooding, and metamorphosis may occur in as little as two weeks. There are five more *Scaphiopus* species found in the USA and Mexico, all requiring similar care.

Common Eurasian Spadefoot
Pelobates fuscus

In Europe, northern Africa, and western Asia, the spadefoots are represented by four species, the best known being the common Eurasian spadefoot, found in lowland western central and eastern Europe and extending into Asia as far as southern Siberia and the northern Caucasus. This is a plump, toad-like anuran with prominent eyes and vertical pupils. Growing to about 8 cm (3.25 in), it is mainly buff in color, marked with blotches and stripes of light brown. Requires similar accommodation to Couch's spadefoot, but with cooler temperatures and greater (but not waterlogged!) humidity.

Asian Horned Frog
Megophrys montana

There are seven genera in the subfamily Megophryinae of the family Pelobatidae, the best known of which is probably *Megophrys* with some 22 species. The Asian horned frog, *M. montana*, is a bizarre species with a fleshy

Common Eurasian spadefoot, *Pelobates fuscus*. Frightened members of this genus often exude a garlic odor.

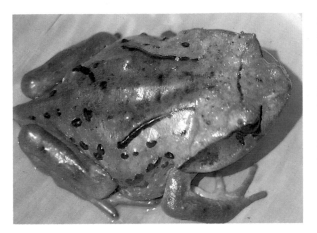

few tropical plants will help maintain the humidity. Fairly constant but relatively cool temperatures (26°C, 79°F) may be maintained year round. Feed on a variety of invertebrates.

"horn" above each eye and another on the tip of the snout. Its color is a mixture of browns and grays which provides good camouflage in its habitat. It is found in southeast Asia in several subspecies, from Thailand through the Malay archipelago to the Philippines. Growing to a length of 12.5 cm (5 in), this species lives in the forest and spends the greater part of the day buried in leaf litter with just the highly camouflaged top of the head (resembling dead leaves) showing. From this position it will lunge at any passing prey.

It should be housed in a tropical type aqua-terrarium with a land/water ratio of two to one. The land area should be provided with a deep layer of leaf litter in which the frogs will hide. The leaf litter must be replaced at regular intervals, as the humid atmosphere required will rapidly aid rotting. A

THE POISON ARROW FROGS OR DENDROBATIDS

Originally classed among the Ranidae, the tiny, colorful members of the family Dendrobatidae are now considered to warrant separate familial classification. With four genera and about 120 species, the dendrobatids are confined to tropical America. Due to their attractive colors and active, diurnal dispositions, these little frogs are highly prized by terrarium keepers. Though not the easiest of terrarium inmates, dedicated enthusiasts now maintain and breed them very successfully, in some cases even on a commercial basis. The bright colors warn prospective predators of the poisonous nature of these frogs, which has been exploited by some tribes of South American Indians who use the poison to tip their arrows. The frogs' body fluids are extracted by heating them over a fire, and the poison is

so potent on the arrow tip that it will quickly subdue a large animal.

Green Poison Arrow Frog
Dendrobates auratus

This species is frequently available to the terrarium keeper. Growing to only 3.5 cm (1.5 in), it is a metallic green color with large, enamel black patches. It occurs from southern Nicaragua to Colombia, where it is an inhabitant of the rainforest and particularly at home among the bromeliads, ferns and other epiphytes of the tree canopy.

Dendrobatids should be housed in a relatively small but tall tropical rainforest terrarium, preferably furnished with tree branches to which water-holding epiphytes are attached. Humidity should be kept very high and temperatures should be maintained between 20 and 29°C (69–84°F). Provide a shallow water dish with pebbles so that the frogs have easy access and egress. Avoid deep water, as the frogs are poor swimmers and could drown. Poison arrow frogs have fascinating breeding habits and, given optimum conditions, captive breeding is frequently successful. After calling and displaying, the male will be approached by a female and the pair will seek out a suitable spawning site, usually on the surface of a leaf. A small clump of eggs is laid by the female and these are fertilized by the male. The male waits near the eggs until they hatch (two to four weeks), then he maneuvers the larvae onto his back and transports them to water, where they are released and continue normal development. Very small bodies of water are used, often in the bracts of a bromeliad or in a hollow of a tree branch. All dendrobatids require similar husbandry.

THE REED FROGS OR HYPEROLIDS

In the past the family Hyperoliidae was considered by most herpetologists to be a subfamily of the Rhacophoridae, but it is now generally agreed that the Hyperoliidae is a family in its own right. The hyperolids consist of three subfamilies, 13 genera and some 220 species found mostly in Africa, with a few species in Madagascar and the Seychelles. The best known members of the family are the reed frogs of the genus *Hyperolius*, of which there are 118 species spread over most of Africa south of the Sahara.

Marbled Reed Frog
Hyperolius marmoratus

Species of reed frog are very similar and have posed taxonomic problems for some time. The marbled reed frog, which occurs in central, eastern and southern Africa, is a particularly "difficult"

species with over 20 subspecies described. The colors are highly variable through greens, browns and yellows, and it may be marbled, blotched, striped or spotted. Growing to about 4 cm (1.5 in). Reed frogs live mainly in vegetation close to marshes, rivers, and ponds. During dry periods they will estivate in the mud. Active by day or night; sometimes fond of sun-bathing on cool mornings.

Reed frogs require a tall terrarium with sturdy grasses or reed-like plants. A high humidity and temperatures of 22–28°C (72–82°F) should be maintained. Feed on a variety of small invertebrates. The species have varied breeding habits. *H. marmoratus* lays its small batches of eggs on the upperside of submerged plants, so a planted

Marbled reed frog, *Hyperolius marmoratus*. This species contains approximately 23 variously patterned subspecies.

61

aqua-terrarium will be necessary for captive breeding.

Running Frog
Kassina senegalensis

An attractive little frog growing to 4 cm (1.5 in), the running frog is a member of the subfamily Kassininae of the family Hyperoliidae. It is usually marked with light brown and black stripes, though color and pattern is highly variable. Largely terrestrial, it tends to run rapidly across the substrate but is capable of hopping if necessary. Found in eastern and southeastern Africa.

Requires a small, tropical rainforest type terrarium with mossy substrate and a few suitable plants. High humidity should be maintained, and temperature of around 26°C (79°F) is recommended. Feed on a variety of small invertebrates.

THE ESCUERZOS

No book about frogs can fail to mention the leptodactylid escuerzos of South America. The family Leptodactylidae contains four subfamilies, 50 genera, and over 750 species. The escuerzos in the subfamily Ceratophryinae are probably the most spectacular and are often kept in the terrarium.

Running frog, *Kassina senegalensis.* **As its common name indicates, this species prefers running to jumping but can hop to it when necessary.**

The escuerzos are also called horned frogs. In some areas, in fact, the name "escuerzo" is never applied to the horned frogs.

Ornate Horned Frog
Ceratophrys ornata

Sharing the genus with six other similarly spectacular species, the

It is a burrowing species which is brought into activity and breeding by seasonal rains. It is a remarkably powerful, fearless frog which can overpower and swallow creatures almost its own size, including small mammals, birds, reptiles, and other frogs. It requires a terrarium with medium humidity,

Ornate horned frog, *Ceratophrys ornata*. The appetite of this species is second to none. Don't let the serenity of this fellow fool you! This is a small juvenile in which the horns have not yet developed.

ornate horned frog or escuerzo has a large head and a huge gape; there is a fleshy "horn" over each eye, and the hindlimbs are relatively short. It has bony, tooth-like projections in the lower jaw and it is capable of giving a painful bite. Growing to a length of 17.5 cm (7 in), this species is found in the pampas regions of Argentina, Uruguay, and Brazil.

deep substrate, and a water dish for bathing. Daytime temperature should be about 27°C (81°F), reduced by a few degrees at night. Feed on a variety of large invertebrates, including earthworms and snails. Even specimens of similar size should never be kept together, and on no account keep larger and smaller specimens together!

Index

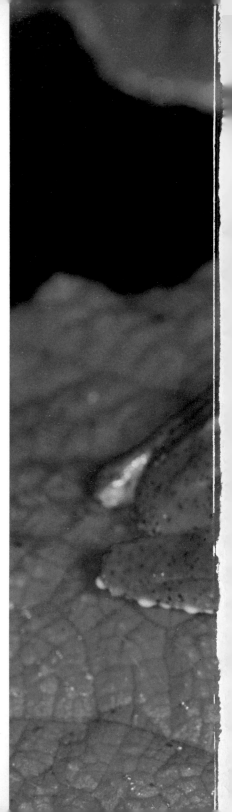